Realistic Personal Growth

Realistic Personal Growth

Table Of Contents

Foreword

Chapter 1:
Healthy Abundance Mindset

Chapter 2:
Meditation

Chapter 3:
Goal Setting

Chapter 4:
Center Yourself

Chapter 5:
Get Over Your Fear

Chapter 6:
Be Grateful

Chapter 7:
Visualize

Wrapping Up

Foreword

This book will help you make witting decisions in your personal development journey and bravely follow up. This means bearing the maturity to take a hundred percent responsibility for your wellness, your vocation, your monetary resources, your relationships, your emotions, your habits, and your spiritual notions.

It calls for taking a deep look at yourself, consciously choosing what sort of individual you really are on the inside, and then getting your outside reality to be congruous with your interior being. The goal is to help you accomplish outstanding effectiveness while sustaining inner balance, where your notions, feelings, actions, and skills are all working collectively to produce the life you really want.

These personal development themes will serve as a great start if you're starting off in personal development.

They'll put you on the correct track to be in control of any situation, accomplish goals and become a better individual.

Practical Personal Development

The Most Popular Personal Development Concepts

Chapter 1:

Healthy Abundance Mindset

Synopsis

Don't live in the scarcity mentality.

This is the psychological state where thoughts of rivalry originate. If you know that there is not enough to go around, you'll attempt to rush to take something from somebody else.

There Is Enough

It might be hard for you to think that rivalry is wrong as it is so highly valued in our society. It feels like every politician or other well paid employee thinks that solely by competition you get what you need.

But that's why they're employees. They don't realize that by not participating in competition they'd become independent and free, even as their natural state ought to be.

When you recognize that competition is wrong and quit trying to gain something at other people's expense, you step by step fall into the abundance mentality. You begin to recognize that you are able to get everything you think of, and this assures you that there will constantly be more than enough of everything for everybody.

However what if you still are in scarcity mentality, and don't know how to get out of it? You'll need to introduce a positive affirmation in your daily life. It may sound like this one: I see abundance everyplace. Or it may be put in this way: there's more than enough resources in the world for everybody. Whichever attracts you more.

You'll likewise need to train your eyes not to see what you don't wish to come up in your life. If you wish to eliminate the thoughts of scarcity, direct your care to the manifestations of abundance. Look at lush nature, deluxe cars, singing morning birds, positive and wealthy individuals, royal buildings, whatsoever you affiliate with abundance.

There are a lot of wealth symbols to choose from, it simply depends which symbols constitute riches to you. I may view nature and see the pure proof of abundance on this Earth; yet other people may see abundance symbols by viewing new gadgets and lavish clothes.

When you train your eyes to center on such symbols, you'll begin the originative process in you. Your thinking will absolutely shift as you no longer see poverty manifestations. By always looking at wealth symbols you'll develop desire to become abundant.

As now you easily center on abundance, you'll have no difficulty in producing thoughts of abundance. These thoughts will manifest in your life bringing in everything you deeply thought about.

An abundance mindset tells you that there are constantly new chances and opportunities. This frees much of the pressure you might feel if you have a scarcity mindset that makes you believe that you only got this shot right now. Or makes you feel like a perfect failure simply because you just bumbled and things didn't work out.

An abundance mindset lets you see life in a more long-run perspective. And it may help you better your performance as with it you're producing a lot less pressure and anxieties inside your own brain.

If you have a scarcity mindset then you'll likely take things too seriously. You might think to yourself: "If I fail, the sky will fall". It likely won't, though. But you believe it will, you become excessively nervous and you've produced a self-fulfilling prophecy of failure as your inner, self-created negativity puts obstructions on your path to success.

Chapter 2:
Meditation

Synopsis

Meditation puts down a great foundation to success. It grooms mental soil for the seeds of abundance (if you decide so).

Meditation does away with negative thinking and gets rid of damaging emotions from your head. I'm not precisely sure why that occurs, but it may be because with practice of meditation you get into a lower frequency of brain activity. In that state the cleansing process may occur.

Power Within

You will not do away with all negative thoughts after meditating one time, however with continuous meditation you'll progress to such a state.

You'll notice that following meditation you feel peaceful. There are not a lot of thoughts circling in your brain and you feel harmony inside. I may describe this feeling as though you've been shielded from adverse thoughts, events and additional damaging occurrences. You feel calm and good.

Occasionally you will get into deep meditation (theta state). You'll get so disengaged from your brain that you'll get aligned with the universe and that will cause you to get a flush of awesome ideas.

That occurs to me really frequently as I've been meditating for a while. Awesome ideas simply flow to you and you achieve those 'wow' moments where you can't believe that you became aware of such an astonishing thought.

I likewise get reminders with meditation of what I ought to do to accomplish some certain goal. It's like the consciousness that I recognize precisely what I ought to do and keeps reminding me of things I'd forget otherwise.

As soon as you begin implementing this personal development notion, you'll get less stressed and eventually you will not get strained at all. Damaging events won't affect you as much because you'll care less about them. Your chief concentration will be on matters that are great and valuable.

You'll begin feeling joy for no apparent cause. You'll catch yourself in the instants of perfect peace and happiness. It will appear that nothing is wrong in this creation and that you're the happiest individual in the world. This is a magical state that meditation produces. Such state ought to be a natural state for everybody, but to most individuals this state is out of the question to get into because of all the negativeness in their minds.

With additional practice of meditation, your intuition will heighten. You'll acquire stronger feelings from inside warning you or spurring you to take some action. You ought to never brush off such signs as they'll only help you to accomplish more and become a better individual.

You'll understand what foods are great for you and what foods harm you. Naturally, this won't come instantly. It might take some time, around two- six months of meditation for a few. You might stop eating meat and other foods. That's because your body tells you that you've been polluting yourself with food you don't require.

The most crucial change that you'll go through is clear thinking. Because you don't have so many damaging thoughts in your brain, you'll begin seeing clean-cut picture of any given situation. You'll understand precisely what to do and how to go about any given state of affairs.

Chapter 3:
Goal Setting

Synopsis

Definite goals assist one important purpose. They keep you proactive. With no goals, you respond to conditions and events. Outside things control you. With goals, you produce your own conditions and events. Therefore you get to be a master of your destiny.

By adjusting goals you keep advancing and bettering your life. You are able to only reach destination if you specify it. Setting goals is the procedure to do that. You will not stagnate if you keep working with this personal development notion.

Get A Plan

Arranging goals lets you accomplish more comfort in life. The chief error individuals make is that they set goals to accomplish happiness. Happiness can't be the object of your goal. Happiness is something you have within you all the time. Perhaps you have not attained it yet, but it's there.

These general hints are organized in a sequence that will support you from considering your goals to really accomplishing them. Don't forget, these are only hints, take what you like and try it out for a while to see what works better for you. Don't make your goals "oughts" but "wants".

Utilize a journal to track your goals journey where you might keep daily or weekly records of your progress including affirmations, winners, appreciations for your hard work, honors, resistances, obstacles, and so forth. Utilize your goals journal to write goals first and to rewrite them over time. Utilize it to break your goals into steps. Critique your progress on a regular basis and jot some notes.

It's very crucial to get yourself into an inspired, positive and relaxed state prior to writing goals. A few ideas for getting yourself into a positive state include: Meditation, hearing inspiring music, reading something fun or funny, watching an amusing movie, taking a walk in a beautiful place, exercise, or prayer.

After getting into a great mental and emotional state, begin your brainstorming. Write all likely goals quickly with no editing or criticism. You may review and prioritize later; right now you lack to be as originative as you can be.

Here are a number of likely areas of your life to consider when you're developing your goals list: job, financial, relationship, loved ones, home, friends, personal development, wellness, appearance, possessions, fun and recreation, travel, spiritual, self-respect and service/community.

Goals fall under variable periods of time like: Immediate goals, 30 day goals, 6 month goals, 1 year goals, 5 years, 10 years or more farsighted. Make certain you may achieve what you want in the time frame you arranged.

When authoring your goal, state it like it has already occurred. Put your goals in words that presume that you already have accomplished them. For instance, "I now have a new car."

To get you passionate, invested and motivated, add emotional language to your composed goals. Here's an illustration "I absolutely adore and am energized about my beautiful new house in the hills" which is much more passionate than "I like my new house".

As your subconscious manifests things literally, you need to compose specific detailed goals. Utilize language that's clear in describing exactly what it is you wish

Compose in favorable terms rather than negative ones.

Check in with yourself to make certain that you're considering what you truly want. Frequently we try to please other people at our own expense. You won't be successful attempting to reach the goals your parents, spouse or other acquaintances or relatives wish for you.

Think about your most crucial values and beliefs when developing your goals. For example if you value freedom, your goal might be to be self-employed. If security is what you value, you might want to work for the government where layoffs rarely occur.

Pick goals that you may really reach in a fair amount of time. After you've brainstormed, one way to prioritize is to put the peak priority goals at ten out of a possible ten points and the least crucial at one out of ten.

Break every goal down into manageable blocks producing a step-by-step plan to accomplish it. For instance, if you require a new automobile, first decide precisely what color, model, year, and brand you need. Write this down in your goals journal. Then write the particular steps you need to get to your goal like.

Chapter 4:
Center Yourself

Synopsis

Center on correct things. You ought to provide your undivided attention to things that will lead you to success. So rather than spending time doing things that eliminate your chances of success (like watching television) you ought to center on taking steps that will get you quicker to your destination.

You ought to always strive to be pro-active and make things occur. Being reactive causes you to lose centering as you're busy responding to events and conditions being thrown at you.

You ought to attempt not to get caught up with too many things. I'd suggest eliminating insignificant ones and centering on those tasks that will benefit you most. You might need to study the 80/20 rule to get better understanding of how to achieve this.

Remaining focused may be really hard.

This leads to the question on how to remain centered on results we would like to effect, and to keep the brain right on target.

Get Focused

Exert your self-control! It's the most difficult thing in the world to remain centered, but you must force your thoughts to quit straying and return to your point.

Find a purpose to help drive you. We commonly lack motivation or a purpose. Have you ever believed that a purpose is like a thrust simply like fuel for an auto? Without a reason that's big enough, you'll hardly make it. If the purpose is huge enough, then the how always handles itself. Failure isn't even a condition.

Clear up your goal. Is it the million dollars you have in mind or is it the boat you are able to purchase if you achieve the goal? Work towards your stated reason in incremental steps - boat today, a million bucks tomorrow.

Repeat a "focus mantra." What you consider is what you set up, even as explained in the Law of Attraction. Your brain is affectionately absorbed with the boat. You read about it, you daydream about it, you look in papers, and you travel to boat stores, and slowly but certainly produce enough thought energy in that pervasive thought to materialize all the things, individuals, chances and cash essential to bring the boat into your life.

Along the way, you didn't dream of having 1 million bucks, you dreamed of the boat as your first centered goal. The notion of the boat becomes real to you in an emotionally charged up way that the million bucks doesn't yet.

Make sure your want for the purpose is strong enough. The most crucial question to ask before you attempt to accomplish any goal is, do you truly have a strong want to make it, a powerful purpose that propels you, that magical gleam in your eyes when you consider it, the certainty to make it? If not, the work will be futile. Simply search deeper and keep seeking that which truly sparks you.

Don't be frightened to dream a huge dream. To keep your brain centered you need large, bold goals. The greater your purpose the less trouble you'll have to accomplish what you have in mind.

Take a break every now and then. This helps you keep centering and refresh your mind. It's advocated you take a 5 minute break each half-hour of work.

Know where you wish to be and how long will this take you? One ought to have ideal short, middle and long-run goals at the back of one's brain. Short-run goals might involve a matter of a couple of months or longer. Endeavor to accomplish and do your best inside a required time frame. This helps cut down complacency and likewise wards off procrastination.

Constantly remember that procrastination is the stealer of time. Keep away from delaying any of your actions by leaving affairs to be done for tomorrow, next week, next month and so forth. Instead have them done today and move on to the following project.

Chapter 5:
Get Over Your Fear

Synopsis

Fearful individuals are never successful. Their fear keeps them from succeeding and becoming what they wish to become. Fear constantly stops progress and stalls individuals.

The fastest way to carry out this personal development idea is by confronting fear. All the same, the simplest way to do away with fear is by understanding that you're in control of everything.

You always manifest your principal mental state. The world you see around you is the expression of how you feel inside. When you comprehend this you will not fear anything as you'll know that you are able to produce everything you wish by altering your mental state.

Be Real

In order to defeat your fear and make it trivial, you have to either make it littler or make your dreams bigger.

When I initially began making a living on my own, I had no idea what I was doing, and I was coping with my own mind-ghosts for the first time.

It's solely in hindsight that I'm able to see what got me through it all. Even while I didn't know precisely what steps to take, it was my single-mindedness that kept me proceeding. I was besieged by my own fear; however I knew what I wanted, so I continued.

Remember, you're in charge of your brain and what goes on inside. Have a deep look at your ideas and see how you're looking at what you wish and what you don't wish.

You might see them, hear them, or feel them, it does not matter which. The crucial thing is that you learn to enlarge what you wish, and shrink what you don't wish.

I'm not talking about brushing aside the bad stuff in your brain, simply making it insignificant for now; you are able to always reverse the procedure later if you wish.

Whatever you feel may be altered. How you feel it may be altered. You're in total control. The only issue is that most individuals aren't willing to claim their power and take responsibility.

Acceptance

The initial time I was asked to do an audio interview. I was anxious, however I knew that in order to achieve my goal, it was inevitable. I had to do it eventually. Thinking like this quieted me and got me pumped-up about doing the interview.

I was considering what I wanted. It doesn't matter if you're considering making a living doing what you adore or simply desiring to have an in demand blog, whatever makes you tick is great.

This is among the chief ways I defeat my own fears day in and day out. I admit that they are there. I look at where I wish to go, and I move ahead, without thinking much, as if I already know where I have to go, there's no reason to second-guess, and it will simply hold me up.

It works for me. Regardless how afraid I am, if I'm always truthful with myself. I know where I wish to go, and I know what I need to do to get there. Any fear is trivial if it's holding me back. It's a waste of time.

Everybody deals with fear, but the successful individuals take action and are willing to deal with failure and whatever foul things might occur.

The only downside with my procedure is that it doesn't work on matters I'm not passionate about. For instance, I'm a little bit grossed out by insects, spiders and the like, but I've no motivation to do away with that fear as it's not relevant for me.

How to Make Your Fears Trivial

By now, I'm certain you're already acquainted with how you are able to overcome your fears and make them trivial, but there's still room to make it easier.

If a fear emerges, consider where you want to go and if you're moving in the correct direction. If you resolve you're moving in the correct direction, recognize the fear and continue moving forward.

This procedure calls for courage to begin with, but when you're comfortable with it, it gets easier to believe that it works.

Why is it that when you walk down the street and run into a sign that states "construction, stay out", you directly consider the best way to get around it and continue moving forward, but when you're heading for a more satisfying life and something comes in your way, you stop dead?

It's because of your disciplining, programming and the affiliations you've made in your life. Everything may be changed. Remember, you have the ability to do whatever you wish. There are no excuses.

Every time I confront one of my fears, it shrivels and finally disappears. The most difficult part is doing it the first couple times. To muster up the courage to get going, I look at the options of buckling under to my fear and moving through it. Life nearly always looks greater when you confront your fears.

If I buckle under to my fear, I'll live a life of sorrow. If I confront my fear, I'll continue growing and moving toward a more fulfilling life. A rough illustration, but I think you are able to see how I frame matters in my own brain.

You have to discover a way to incite yourself. It's begins by taking action and learning how your brain works. It's simple to believe that your brain, your thoughts and your feelings are in command, but if that's real, why is it that you're able to observe your thoughts and feelings when you're totally present?

How can your thoughts be in control if there is an overseer watching them? They can't. Breathe, relax and be in the now, and you become the observer.

Chapter 6:
Be Grateful

Synopsis

Gratitude brings you more and greater things you're grateful for. This is because the cosmos reacts to your gratitude in giving more of what you're thankful for.

Being grateful is the reason, getting more of what you're giving thanks for is the effect. Each action has a particular reaction; consequently gratitude has this particular reaction that may never be changed.

Gratitude is a really powerful force that reaches the object to which you're thanking immediately. It likewise gets you into a harmonious state aligned with the cosmos. This puts you in a flow of life causing you to develop success effortlessly.

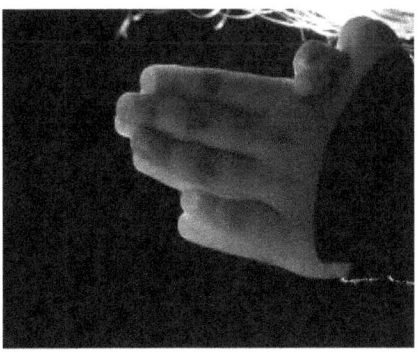

Give Thanks

Among the best things that you are able to do is to have gratitude; for everything that you have, everything that you've done, for all the individuals in your life, and for the procedure of unfolding and development. It's crucial. Gratitude is among the higher vibrations in this life and it draws in a super-flow in your life.

Without gratitude one may get arrogant, and isolated. Till you truly look at all that you have, and treasure all that you've been given, things may be non-meaningful. Did you have anything to do with your appearance? Or your eye color? Or an utterly healthy body? Or where you were born? Not at all.

Have thankfullness for all that has been produced for you. Think, that you are able to see distinctly the trees and beauty around you, that you are able to take a breath of fresh air, that today and just where you are, you're capable of so many things. Be thankful for the knowledge that you have been presented or that you've learned.

Be thankful that you've so many individuals who love you deeply and profoundly. Be thankful for each experience that has strengthened you and shaped you into the individual you'll become. It's easy to say that "I did this all", but there are so many individuals who have contributed both knowingly and inadvertently to your success, your emotional support, balance in your life, and your power. There's a force right now in your life that holds you on track; be witting of that.

There are individuals that you meet who have a deep affect on you in one meeting. There are others that you formulate relationships with over time. There are instructors who are great, but you don't truly know their affect till many years later. There are guides who have been fortunately placed on your path at simply the correct moment, to comfort or fortify you. There are several who respect you simply because of who you are, what you state, and how you've touched their lives. Have thankfullness for all of these.

With a spirit of gratitude, you will be able to call things to you before they've unfolded. That gratitude states to the universe that you're open to getting and have already received something in your heart. You put into action a reason and effect that the universe produces according to your prompting and gratitude.

The gratitude pulls it in like a magnet. When you wish to produce and receive, thank the cosmos for bringing it to you before it occurs and it will be manifest for you. "Thanks for healing me." "Thanks for bringing in the correct person for me." "Thanks for my home with the big windows."

Put it out with gratitude and remain open for it and it is on its way. It may take some time as just the correct set of conditions have to come together to provide you the absolute best results.

Oh, and one matter about gratitude, you have to feel it. You can't just pretend. When you have gratitude there's a power shift change to a greater vibration in your body that interacts with the universal power.

Without that shift modification of energy, you will not manifest the way that you wish. Without thankfullness very likely there will be a stagnancy of anything new that might come for you. And occasionally you experience a reversal, as if you're not grateful for what you have, it begins to leave.

Practice gratitude today. Take nothing for granted. This moment is so brief. Make a list of 10 things right now that you're grateful for. Say it or read it aloud daily. It only takes a few minutes to alter your thinking, and therefore your receiving.

Chapter 7:
Visualize

Synopsis

This personal development idea will keep you advancing in life and presenting you clues and opportunities to accomplish what you're visualizing.

If you bear in mind one image for a while without being distracted, you'll bring that picture into manifestation.

After visualization you might begin seeing clues as to what you have to do to achieve your desires. Make sure to act on them to bring your visualization into truth.

You ought to be aware that this personal development idea doesn't work alone. If your constant psychological state is negative, 10 minutes a day of visualization won't bring you success.

This is because when you visualize your wants, your negative frame of mind serves like an obstacle preventing you from acquiring what you wish. What you visualized has already manifested in the intangible world, yet the manifestations are precluded from reaching you because of your mind.

Therefore if you're still negative, you first off need to work on your mental state. Once your brain becomes neutral or positive, visualization will act as the acceleration of the manifestation of your goals.

See It

Write down everything that you ever wanted. Plow ahead, have a blast! No limits here. Simply suppose that you have your fairy godmother that may grant you any wish you call for and you are able to have utterly anything that you ever wanted.

Think impossible? Think not! Simply write down whatsoever comes to your mind that you want, things, individuals, and places you wish to go, things you wish to do, individuals you wish to meet, your dreams and so forth. Put down at least fifty things that you always wanted.

Here's the part where you have to do more work. However did I mention that it's fun? Have that list of things you forever desired? Read through the list of things that you desired, consider them and then prioritize them.

Following, purchase a board, it may be a sticky board or a cork board or even simply cardboard. You truly just need a board where you are able to stick pictures on. Get out your magazines and scissors and begin snipping pictures that you are able to relate to your list of things you desire.

Once you've sufficient pictures, stick those pictures up on board you've prepared. Voila! Your vision board is now set up!

Now look at your vision board a lot and really see yourself in the situations you want to bring about. Remember to stay in a positive mindset.

Wrapping Up

Discipline is really crucial to the procedure of self improvement. Your entire life will be so much greater if your conquer yourself.

When you master self-control, you will become a totally different individual. You will understand so much more than you understood previously. You will be able to arrange goals and really accomplish them, your fears will be gone and an entire new life will be ahead of you.

How to go about it? You first of all need to comprehend that you're not your emotions. You're not your thinking. You're not your ego. You are part of the total consciousness. Thinking, self-control and emotions were given to you as tools to utilize in this life. You're not any of these things.

When you comprehend this and control all your aspects, you'll conquer yourself. You'll become totally disciplined and will be able to accomplish whatever you want.

Individuals commonly desire fast results, but when they find out what is involved in accomplishing them, they are put off by the entire process of self improvement. If you feel this way, attempt to recognize what awesome benefits you will get when you make huge steps in personal development.

Now it is up to you to choose if you still wish to accelerate personal development. This is a really exciting path, but it does call for work on your part.

www.ingramcontent.com/pod-product-compliance
Lightning Source LLC
LaVergne TN
LVHW020742090526
838202LV00057BA/6185